Preparing for a Career
in the
Legal Profession

Laurie Robinson Haden

Preparing for a Career in the Legal Profession
Copyright © 2024 by Laurie Robinson Haden
All Rights Reserved

Cover Designer: TBD
Interior Designer: Dr. Melissa Caudle
Photos: Stock Nation Club and 123rf.com used with permission

Paperback ISBN:979-8-89401-110-3
eBook ISBN: 979-8-89401-000-7

TABLE OF CONTENTS

Chapter 1

What Is a Lawyer?

A lawyer is a licensed professional who practices law and advises individuals, businesses, governmental agencies, and organizations.

To become a lawyer, you will need specialized training in law, which usually requires seven years of education after completing high school (four years of college and three years of law school).

Upon completing law school, you will receive a law degree known as a Doctorate of Jurisprudence (J.D.). Next, to practice law, you will need to pass a state bar examination. Once you pass the bar, you will be admitted to the State Bar, receive a license to practice law, and begin practicing law.

As a lawyer, you will have countless opportunities to pursue your passions. Like the medical field, the law has a robust list of specialty fields that range from intellectual property to estate planning and probate.

There are many avenues to pursue, including family law, technology law, criminal law, civil rights law, real estate law, and corporate law.

What Does a Lawyer Do?

A lawyer is a zealous advocate for his/her client and works to ensure justice and the rule of law. Lawyers provide legal advice, guidance, and counsel for their clients.

If you watch legal dramas on television, such as *Judge Judy, The Lincoln Lawyer,* and *Law & Order*, you have seen a glimpse of what lawyers do — from questioning witnesses to appearing in courtrooms. However, this is only a small aspect of what a lawyer does.

Lawyers perform various functions, and the duties differ depending on the specialized area of the law. Most spend significant time gathering information and facts through research, writing memoranda to summarize their findings and legal issues, analyzing case law, and devising strategies to help clients receive the best possible outcomes. Lawyers may also be involved in drafting contracts, reviewing contracts, negotiating settlements, mediating disputes, and attending trial.

Chapter 2

Why You Should Become a Lawyer

Reasons to Enter the Legal Profession

There are many reasons people enter the legal profession. Some people are simply fascinated by complex and critical thinking. Others love to talk and argue. Many people are motivated by their personal experiences with the law that have impacted them, either positively or negatively. There are several other reasons why you should be a lawyer.

1. **It's a Way to Pay It Forward and Give Back**: The practice of law provides the opportunity to help others, make a difference, and give back to the community. Your legal expertise will help people understand their legal rights and can help them navigate through the complexities of the legal system to protect their rights.

2. **The Practice of Law Is an In-Demand Field**: In a professional sense, a law degree can facilitate a range of employment opportunities. It is a high-demand field. According to the U.S.

3

Bureau of Labor Statistics, jobs for lawyers are predicted to increase by 10% between 2021 and 2031. Opportunities will increase with emerging legal issues, such as intellectual property, privacy and cybersecurity, and artificial intelligence, to name a few.

3. **Over 70 Fields to Specialize**: Even better, this flexible career offers dozens of specialties (as listed above) and opportunities to work in different settings. You could join a law firm, work for the government, serve as corporate counsel for a corporation, or begin your own law firm.

4. **You Have a Chance to Shape Policies:** If you are passionate about the environment or social issues, you can pursue a job that allows you to stand up for your personal beliefs. If you want to help families going through divorces or child custody disputes, you can focus on this area of law. The opportunities are endless.

5. **Financial Stability**: The practice of law, depending on your specialty, can provide

financial stability. According to the 2020 U.S. Bureau of Labor Statistics, the median income of an attorney is $126,930. Salary will depend on your practice area, location, and economy. If you decide to start your career at a major law firm, your salary could be $250,000 annually. If you rise through the ranks to become a partner at one of the top firms in America, your annual salary could range from $500,000 to $2 million **per year**. Good lawyers also earn a better-than-average living and enjoy high social influence, thanks to their knowledge, experience, and skill.

Chapter 3

What Tests Are Required to Attend Law School?

What Is the LSAT?

You have likely taken a standardized test in elementary school, such as the IOWA Assessments or CogAT. In high school, you may have already taken the SAT or ACT.

Many law schools require the Law School Admission Test (LSAT), a standardized test that helps determine your eligibility for admission. This half-day test includes around 100 multiple-choice questions and a writing sample. You do not need to know anything about the law to take the LSAT. Instead, it is designed to determine whether you have the skill set necessary to excel in legal studies. There are other criteria for admission to law school, and some universities accept other types of standardized tests, but many schools still require this exam.

Best Practices to Prepare for the LSAT

The LSAT has three scored multiple-choice sections: reading comprehension, analytical reasoning, and logical reasoning. It also includes an unscored, multiple-choice section. A separate written portion is not scored but could still impact your application.

You will have 35 minutes to complete each multiple-choice section. You can receive a score between 120 and 180. The median score is around 150. To get into the top 10 law schools, such as Harvard, Yale, and Stanford, you will likely need a score of 170 or above.

NOTE: Law schools also look at how well-rounded a student is, so make sure you involve yourself in leadership roles at school and community service activities while also building your work experience in high school and college with relevant summer internships.

The Law School Admission Council (LSAC) makes and administers the test. You can visit the LSAC website to get an overview of the test, see sample questions, and take practice exams that allow you to gauge your baseline and determine where you need more preparation. Before you take the test, finding some LSAT prep books and practice exams to study and test yourself at home is a good idea. You can also find a range of programs offering test prep services with the aid of online learning or personalized tutoring. Kaplan Test Prep and the Princeton Review are two of the most popular test prep courses.

It is recommended that you study consistently for six months with a regular study schedule before the test, so you have plenty of time to get familiar with the test, practice materials, and test-taking strategies.

Other Requirements

In addition to the LSAT, law schools may have various other requirements. As part of your application, you will need to graduate from college, meet GPA requirements, and submit a personal statement. You will also need glowing letters of recommendations, ideally from professors, mentors, or other authority figures.

Depending on the schools you are interested in, you might take the Graduate Record Examinations (GRE) in lieu of the LSAT. This standardized exam, designed to measure aptitude for abstract thinking across a range of subjects, has become more widely accepted by law schools.

Chapter 4

Courses to Take to Prepare for the Study of Law

There are several majors and subjects that can prepare you for the study of law.

History

No law study is complete without understanding the legal system's history and the events surrounding its development. In addition to learning valuable information about the progression of the U.S. and its ruling systems, history courses help you develop essential skills you will need as a lawyer. These include research, reasoning, writing, and sifting through diverse information from fairly broad subject matters.

Political Science

Political science focuses mainly on the theory and practice of politics and government. This knowledge is useful for understanding how and why laws are made, enforced, and changed over time. Classes in political science may explore information about local, state, national, and international governance, and political systems. The benefit for law students, particularly, is that knowledge about the executive and legislative branches enhances understanding of the judiciary and its complexities and influences.

As a lawyer, it is important to see every possible angle. Knowing how politics, public sentiment, and other factors contribute to legislation and the decisions made by courts can only help you when developing legal strategies.

English

English includes subjects like vocabulary and grammar, reading comprehension, and writing — whether essays, fiction, or technical content. Many English courses focus on communicating effectively, drawing connections, and creating well-thought-out arguments. Laws are all about how language is used and interpreted, and you need a strong background in English to succeed as a lawyer.

Philosophy

Philosophy is another area of study that is unquestionably helpful in the legal profession. This subject is concerned with understanding fundamental truths, and it covers everything from logic and reasoning to arguments and fallacies to ethics.

If you plan on becoming a lawyer, no two subjects are more valuable to the daily demands of your job than English and philosophy. With a strong background in these two areas, you will be well-prepared to approach complex situations and data sets, analyze and interpret information, evaluate evidence, and formulate logic-based arguments.

Ultimately, the strongest legal argument wins, and using the right language is essential, whether drafting a contract, deposing a witness, or making your case to a jury.

Public Administration

The law is tied to public administration. This field focuses on officials and organizations that protect and serve the public and advance the common good.

Public administration could include urban planning, public health, education, social services, and public safety. Public administrators are tasked with upholding laws, ensuring public health and safety, addressing discrimination and civil rights issues, managing budgets, and much more.

Why is this an important subject for law students? First of all, your law degree might lead you to a career in public administration. You might want to become a federal agent, work in local government, or meet the legal needs of a nonprofit organization. These are all public service jobs.

In addition, public administration has a strong bearing on the law and vice versa. Public administration operates within the framework of the law, but it can also influence how laws are created, interpreted, and enforced.

As a lawyer, you are likely to frequently cross paths with public administrators and organizations, and understanding how they work and intersect with the law is incredibly important.

Sociology and Psychology

A major in psychology can provide a valuable understanding of human behavior and mental processes, which can be applied in areas such as criminal law and family law. Similarly, a sociology major offers insights into the social dynamics and structures that influence legal issues, such as inequality, discrimination, and social justice. Both majors provide a strong foundation for understanding the complexities of the human experience and its intersection with the law.

Economics

Economics provides a strong foundation about how markets and incentives work, which helps with antitrust law, business law, and regulatory law. The analytical and quantitative skills developed in economics are highly transferable to legal analysis.

STEM (Science, Technology, Engineering, and Math)

STEM majors provide a strong foundation for success in law school by fostering critical thinking, analytical skills, and problem-solving abilities. The demanding coursework in science, technology, engineering, and math nurtures a logical and systematic approach, which is invaluable for conducting thorough legal research, analyzing complex legal issues, and formulating persuasive arguments. These subject matters also provide a great foundation for intellectual property law, AI law, patent law, and healthcare law.

Chapter 5

Choosing a Law School

When selecting a law school, several factors need to be taken into consideration, from the programs and career services offered to the cost of attending the school. You should visit the law school, sit in on a few classes, talk to the students and professors, and determine whether you like the school, campus, and atmosphere. Here are some important factors that you may consider.

Cost of Tuition

The average cost of tuition for law school is $50,000 per year. If you multiply that number by three years, a law degree's tuition average is $150,000. Ivy League law schools, like Stanford, Harvard, and Yale, charge around $80,000 annually in tuition fees. Consider how much you will have to take on in student loan debt. Make sure to apply for scholarships or grants to help reduce the cost. Also, if you are concerned about the cost of law school, consider attending a law school in your state to benefit from in-state tuition.

Location

Location is an important factor because it impacts your cost of living. You will have to account for living costs for rent, food, utilities, and more. The law school's location can also affect opportunities for internships and work opportunities post-graduation.

Programs

Location and cost are not everything. You also need to think about the programs the law school offers.

Overall, your main focus should be finding the right program that suits your interests and strengths. By the time you complete your undergraduate degree, you might have some idea of what areas of law interest you or will be best suited to your particular talents.

Look for programs that offer the coursework and opportunities that will set you on your preferred career path. Many schools have programs that focus on subject matter expertise, such as international law, patent law, and civil rights. These programs will likely have what you are looking for, but you will have to do some research to narrow it down to the program that best meets your needs.

In addition, programs and activities that may be of interest and that will build your leadership skills and make you a well-rounded student include:

- Legal clinics
- Law review and journals
- Mock trial
- Pro bono programs
- Externships
- Study abroad programs
- Student government
- Law student affinity groups

Career Services

The career services that a law school offers play a crucial role, providing priceless resources and opportunities for networking with alumni. The career services office also helps with resume writing, review, and interview preparation, which, importantly, will lead to internships and job placement in the summer and post-graduation.

Overall Compatibility

You may be willing to compromise on certain aspects. For example, an undesirable location could be more attractive if the school fits your budget or offers you a scholarship. However, you should not compromise on your preferred degree program, since it will impact your career options going forward.

Attending a prestigious school is a top priority for some students. Maybe you are a "legacy" and want to attend the institution other family members have graduated from. You may want access to the networking and job opportunities an institution can offer. You may also want a small, hands-on, nurturing environment. Weighing all these factors will help you find the best fit.

While many students work during an undergrad program, you should prepare to focus on your studies during an intensive law program. However, some law schools do cater to working professionals, offering part-time or online courses.

Financial Support Available for Students

The thought of attending law school can be daunting. It requires several years of undergraduate and graduate study. Schooling can be expensive, especially if you are accepted into top universities.

The good news is that many scholarships are available to those interested in the study of law. For example, undergraduate students who plan on taking the LSAT can apply for the Blueprint LSAT Law School Scholarship, a $20,000 award.

If you want to see what the legal profession is like before you start school, you could apply for the Weil Legal Innovators (WLI) program. In this program, you defer your first year of law school to partner with a WLI nonprofit for a paid public service legal fellowship.

There are also a range of diversity-based scholarships available for law students. The NAACP Legal Defense and Educational Fund offers different scholarships. Most notably, the Marshall-Motley Scholars Program fully funds law school scholarships for aspiring civil rights lawyers prepared to advocate for Black communities. The program also provides internship and fellowship opportunities.

Chapter 6

Different Fields of Law

There are many different fields of study within the legal profession. This means that you can explore your interests and decide to help people who are facing specific situations.

Some fields of law that may interest you are:

1. Administrative Law
2. Admiralty and Maritime Law
3. Adoption Law
4. Antitrust Law
5. Appellate Law
6. Aviation Law
7. Bankruptcy Law
8. Business Law
9. Civil Rights Law
10. Commercial Law
11. Communications Law
12. Constitutional Law
13. Construction Law
14. Consumer Law
15. Contract Law
16. Corporate Law
17. Criminal Law
18. Cyber Law
19. Disability Law
20. Divorce Law
21. Education Law
22. Elder Law
23. Employment Law
24. Energy Law
25. Entertainment Law
26. Environmental Law
27. Estate Planning
28. Family Law
29. Financial Services Law
30. Food and Drug Law
31. Gaming Law
32. Health Law
33. Immigration Law
34. Indigenous Law

35. Information Technology Law
36. Insolvency Law
37. Insurance Law
38. Intellectual Property Law
39. International Law
40. Labor Law
41. Land Use and Zoning Law
42. Litigation Law
43. Media Law
44. Medical Malpractice Law
45. Mergers and Acquisitions Law
46. Military Law
47. Native American Law
48. Natural Resources Law
49. Nonprofit Law
50. Occupational Safety and Health Law
51. Patents Law
52. Personal Injury Law
53. Privacy Law

54. Probate Law
55. Product Liability Law
56. Professional Liability Law
57. Property Law
58. Public Interest Law
59. Real Estate Law
60. Regulatory Law
61. Securities Law
62. Social Security Law
63. Sports Law
64. Tax Law
65. Technology Law
66. Telecommunications Law
67. Tort Law
68. Trade Law
69. Trademarks Law
70. Transportation Law
71. Trusts Law
72. Utilities Law
73. Venture Capital Law
74. Veterans Law
75. Water Law
76. White Collar Crime Law
77. Wills Law
78. Workers' Compensation Law
79. Wrongful Death Law

Even within these broad categories, you may further specialize in certain areas. For example, an attorney in family law could work primarily on cases involving divorce, paternity and child custody, adoption, guardianship, or domestic abuse.

Corporate law exists in literally every type of trade. You could concentrate on working with businesses in the medical, entertainment, manufacturing, sports, travel, or fuel industries, as well as many others. As a corporate lawyer, for example, you may focus on contracts, operations, compliance, intellectual property, or mergers and acquisitions.

The point is that there is no single pathway to becoming a lawyer. You can pursue your own interests and values as part of your profession and enjoy a personally fulfilling career.

Chapter 7

What Are the Various Practice Areas for Law?

Legal Fields

Since laws apply to everyone, including citizens, corporations, and the government, there are endless legal fields to explore.

Couples going through a divorce may need legal help to figure out how to divide their assets fairly or share custody of children. A person who is bitten by his or her neighbor's dog or slips on an icy sidewalk may need to sue the responsible party to cover medical bills.

The FBI needs competent and skilled investigators to build cases against individuals and entities involved in federal crimes. People or businesses might require assistance properly interpreting and complying with tax laws — or fighting unfair taxation.

As you can see, there is no end to the avenues you might explore with a degree in law, which makes it an incredibly flexible career path. When you pursue your interests, you can enjoy a job in law that challenges and fulfills you on both a personal and professional level.

The Most Competitive Fields

Some of the most competitive legal fields also happen to be the most complicated. Unsurprisingly, they are also among the highest paying. Corporate law, and specifically complex litigation, can offer exciting career opportunities, but the stakes are often higher than average.

As a corporate lawyer, you may be responsible for the health of a corporate entity. You might work with its development and operations, or you might oversee how it complies with rules and regulations or deals with lawsuits.

Since complex litigation could involve multiple parties and large sums of money, corporate lawyers who specialize in this area must be at the top of their game to protect their clients' interests.

Tax law is another field that is incredibly complex. Therefore, good tax lawyers will always be in high demand. Other high-stakes areas of legal practice that tend to attract top talent include:

- Civil Rights
- Criminal
- Environmental
- Healthcare
- Immigration
- Intellectual Property
- Labor
- Sports and Entertainment

Some of these fields pay exceptionally well; others pay less but involve a level of social justice that engages an attorney's core values and beliefs, delivering an entirely different form of payout.

Chapter 8

Emerging Practice Areas

Technology

Technology law centers on existing and emerging technologies. A tech lawyer might work with anything that involves applying scientific knowledge for practical purposes. As a lawyer focused on technology, you have several different options for the interest you want to pursue.

STEM

For example, you might work in the private sector for a technology company like Apple and Google, helping to ensure compliance with changing laws surrounding its products or services. On the other hand, you could work for the government, like the Federal Trade Commission, helping to establish or enforce industry regulations.

Some lawyers work specifically with medical technologies and the many legalities surrounding how they are developed and utilized. Additionally, tech law can overlap with intellectual property law when certain technologies are too similar.

Your interests could play a major role in your career path, opening the door to both professional and personal fulfillment. As a tech lawyer, you have a wide range of specializations to focus on, such as:

- Software and communications
- Wearable devices
- Transportation and aerospace

- Green energy
- Pharmaceuticals and surgical devices

This field of law can be exciting and challenging simply because of the pace at which technology evolves.

Privacy

Privacy law is a complex and evolving field that focuses on the ways in which personal information is gathered, stored, and used. These days, it often overlaps with communications technologies. Like technology law, this growing practice area spans a wide array of industries.

So much of your life exists in a digital format. Information about your finances, healthcare, education, and private life is stored and used in ways you might not know about.

What happens to your financial data when you digitally deposit checks with your phone or send a payment to a friend through Venmo? Where is your medical information stored, and how secure is it? How are social media sites using information about your posts, likes, and shares? What data are they collecting, and who are they selling it to?

Privacy law is all about creating a balance between protecting personal privacy and allowing for the flow of commerce. Like other emerging specialties, this field has job openings in both private and government sectors, providing a range of professional opportunities to explore.

Artificial Intelligence (AI)

Artificial intelligence falls under the broad category of tech law. Because it is so complex, AI is a hot topic in the legal field. The issues surrounding AI pertain not only to specific technologies but also to the ethical challenges of creating programs designed to learn and adapt independently.

While AI is still in its infancy, many assumptions exist about its future. This speculation is not just about intelligent machines that take over the world, either. There are many more probable and potentially risky applications for AI.

Today, surgeons are performing robot-assisted procedures, but one day, computerized surgery could be the norm. One current use of AI that seems relatively harmless has to do with advertising. If you have ever noticed that you are talking about a product and suddenly your phone starts serving you ads for that product, you are seeing AI at work.

The legal ramifications are wide-ranging, with applications in both government and private sectors. This field of law will only become more pressing and complicated.

Chapter 9

What Can You Do with a Law Degree?

With a law degree, you can become a practicing attorney, work in legal research or policy, advocate for justice, or pursue a career in business or government.

Work at a Law Firm

If you plan to work for a law firm, it is likely you will start before you even graduate by taking on internships and working as a summer associate or paralegal.

Associates help more experienced attorneys with research, court filings, and other tasks. In time, you may eventually be promoted to senior associate. At that point, you will manage associates and have your own clients to advise and represent.

Finally, you may be asked to become a partner in the firm. Partners help manage and oversee every aspect of the firm's operations and earn a much higher salary, which, in top firms, can be $2 million a year. You might even branch out and start your own private practice.

Work for a Corporation

Working as an in-house attorney at a corporation like McDonald's or Microsoft provides a dynamic and rewarding legal career. In this role, you serve as a strategic partner to the company, offering legal advice and guidance on a wide range of issues. One of the main advantages of working in-house is the opportunity to deeply understand the company's operations, culture, and objectives. This knowledge allows you to provide customized and proactive legal solutions that align with the company's goals. In-house attorneys collaborate closely with various departments, such as finance, human resources, and compliance, to ensure legal adherence to legal standards and manage risks. You will also have the chance to work on diverse matters, including contract negotiations, intellectual property protection, employment law, regulatory compliance, and litigation management. In-house roles typically offer a better work-life balance compared to positions at law firms, emphasizing the development of long-term relationships and contributing to the company's overall success.

Work in Public Service (Government and Nonprofits)

There are two main routes you could take when it comes to a career in public service: government entities or nonprofit organizations that work for the public good.

Government jobs for legal professionals exist at the local, state, and federal levels. You may also be interested in working in tribal law, particularly if you are a member of a Native American tribe. Within this massive wheelhouse, you could end up working locally as a public defender or become an assistant district attorney or judge.

You might join federal organizations like the FBI, Department of Defense, or Veterans Affairs. Or you could work in social services or public administration. Tax law specialists, policy analysts, and regulatory affairs specialists are also considered public officials.

As a different career path, you might be interested in offering your services to nonprofit organizations that align with your core values and beliefs. Labor unions, civil rights organizations, research institutes, and public charities are all options to explore.

Participate in Politics

Many politicians have law degrees. If you are interested in politics and legislation, a law degree can be a major boon. Maybe you have the charisma and drive to throw your hat into the political ring as a state legislator, mayor, governor, member of Congress, or even President of the United States. You will help create and enforce the laws that govern your city or state — or even the nation.

Understanding the law is an excellent basis for a job in politics. You can get started while you are in law school, or even beforehand, by volunteering with a political campaign to see how the process works or interning with a senator or congressperson during the summer.

You may decide that you do not want to be in the public spotlight as a politician. However, this does not have to stop you from working in politics.

Legal professionals can serve as campaign lawyers, advising on matters like finance law and ethics. Additionally, you could help shape public policy by working in a legislative office for a senator or congressperson. All can be incredibly rewarding careers.

Chapter 10

How Much Money Does a Lawyer Make?

Government

If you decide to pursue a career in government law, you may work for entities at the local, state, or federal level. Jobs in this area of law could include public defender, policy analyst, assistant district attorney, or special agent for a law enforcement agency like the CIA, FBI, or DEA.

These jobs can be exciting and are often high-profile. But as a professional, it is important to know what type of salary you can earn when you bring your legal skills to a government job.

Public defenders acting as attorneys for local or state governments earn an average salary of just over $71,000 per year, while a policy analyst involved in researching and developing public policies could bring in around $73,000 annually.

An assistant prosecutor, or assistant district attorney for the government, enjoys a national average salary of about $96,000 per year, and special agents working as investigators for government agencies earn about $105,000 annually, on average. Salaries may vary by education, experience, and geographic region, among other factors.

Law Firm

There are many different legal fields, and law firms may specialize in one or more. For this reason, salaries can vary widely across law firms. If you work in a law firm, your salary will depend largely on your area of specialization, the relative prestige of the firm, your geographic region, and your qualifications, including education and experience.

For example, the annual mean wage for those working in legal services is just over $166,000, according to the U.S. Bureau of Labor Statistics.

That number bumps up to just over $200,000 for lawyers in California and about $189,000 in New York. Washington, D.C., is even higher, with an annual mean wage of over $226,000 per year. Partners at major law firms may earn between $500,000 and $7,000,000 per year.

Your salary may also depend on your employer. Working for a top law firm versus a private practice, for example, could result in very different salaries. Your position makes a difference, as well; associates will earn less than partners.

Corporate Counsel

Corporate lawyers may work for one or more business entities. They advise their clients on certain legal aspects of business operations.

For example, they may help the company avoid liability, ensure compliance with industry rules and regulations, and represent their employer in lawsuits and other legal matters. Corporate lawyers are also involved in the formation, operation, and governance of companies in keeping with applicable laws.

The median annual salary for a corporate lawyer in the U.S. is nearly $120,000. Base salaries range from about $74,000 to about $205,000. For an entry-level position, you could expect to earn about $100,000 per year, while seasoned lawyers with 20 years of experience under their belt earn $355,000 annually, on average.

Again, corporate law salaries vary widely by region. They could also vary by the type of industry you work in. Lawyers working in publishing earn an average of $235,000 annually, while those in the oil and gas field earn about $206,000 per year.

By comparison, lawyers in individual and family services earn about $80,000 per year, far below the national average for lawyers.

Chapter 11

Fun Things You Can Do to Expose Yourself to the Law

Enjoy Legal Dramas

Americans are fascinated by the multiple workings of their country's legal system.

This fascination has resulted in a wealth of media devoted to the law. Unscripted shows like *Judge Judy, Traffic Court, The People's Court*, and *Divorce Court* have been popular for decades. Legal dramas on television and the big screen, such as *Perry Mason, My Cousin Vinny*, and *12 Angry Men* and, recently, *The Lincoln Lawyer, The Good Wife, The Good Fight*, and *Suits*, have significant viewership.

The popularity of law-related programming has endured. Today, you can enjoy attention to a wide range of streaming content centered on legal practice, including dramas, comedies, and reality shows. And true-crime podcasts in the vein of *Serial* exist.

While these programs do not always accurately represent how real-world lawyers operate, they can be entertaining introductions to the field of law.

Join Speech and Debate

Not all jobs in law require you to make legal arguments, but this can be a crucial task for many lawyers. Skills like logical reasoning and forming compelling arguments will likely serve you well when you plan a career in law.

One of the best ways to do this is by joining your school's speech and debate clubs. You will learn how to make strong arguments with factual, ethical, and persuasive elements. And you will hone and test these skills by debating with your classmates and teams from other schools.

Additionally, public speaking is something that helps you in almost any career, but especially in law. Surveys have shown that as much as 75% of the population suffers from a fear of public speaking. However, as a lawyer or law student, you will likely be called upon to deliver presentations or otherwise speak publicly.

Internships, Conferences, and Immersion Programs

Internships allow you to learn while performing job-related tasks. Externships consist of shadowing a professional or mentor to see what their day-to-day looks like. These are both great ways to understand different job types within the legal field.

Whether you are looking for an introduction to the inner workings of law firms, corporate legal teams, courtrooms, or legislative settings, an internship or externship is a good place to start.

You might work for a legislator or help at a nonprofit that focuses on civil rights, workers' rights, or criminal justice. Or you could end up shadowing a legal professional, gaining valuable insights, and making industry connections along the way.

Many law schools also offer conferences for undergraduate students. These events may feature seminars, workshops, notable speakers, and panels covering timely subjects. Intensive immersion programs typically expose you to a range of professionals within the field to provide an overview of your options.

Chapter 12

Practice Games to Start Thinking Like a Lawyer

Argument Wars

Learning about the law does not have to mean spending all day in a library, pouring over massive books. Thanks to mobile apps and gamification, you can access options that are a lot more fun and portable.

If you are interested in litigation and courtroom drama, you can download *Argument Wars.* This app allows you to argue famous Supreme Court cases, such as *Brown* v. *Board of Education*, *Gideon* v. *Wainwright*, and *Miranda* v. *Arizona*. In a game where the strongest argument wins, you will learn to analyze real-world cases, evaluate the support and reasoning for your argument, and weigh precedents.

Ultimately, you will be tested not only on the strength of your argument but also on how persuasive you can be when delivering it, much like in a real courtroom setting. If you want the opportunity to argue real cases that have helped shape this country, you will find this educational game from iCivics thrilling. It features a user-friendly layout and is available for free download on Apple and Android devices.

Quizlet

A big part of thinking like a lawyer is understanding the law, including legal jargon, important cases, and laws specific to your preferred area of study. *Quizlet* is not a legal app, but it can help with all of your studies, including pre-law and law coursework.

What started as a flashcard app to help students study for quizzes has grown into a much more robust tool for making studying fun. The *Quizlet* learning platform offers flashcards and practice tests in a range of subjects. You can benefit from a responsive AI tutor, and you can even turn your own notes into flashcards.

Even better, users can share their flashcards and knowledge with each other. For example, you can search existing posts for administrative, civil, comparative, constitutional, and criminal law to find flashcard sets and helpful Q and As.

Whether you are already in pre-law or want to get a head start exploring the legal field, this free app offers a powerful study tool.

Chess

Strategy and deductive reasoning are two essential modes of thinking in the field of law, and you do not need law-themed games to develop these cognitive skills. If you want to go old-school when honing critical thinking skills, games like poker and chess are great options.

Chess is about anticipating your opponent's every move and figuring out how to counter their several moves in advance. Succeeding at chess requires knowledge of strategy, probability, and human nature.

For something a little less intense, try a game of *Monopoly* or *Clue*. *Monopoly* is partially a game of chance, but you can also formulate strategies that help you grow your bank and, ultimately, control the board. *Clue,* on the other hand, is a game that centers on deductive reasoning, requiring you to collect facts and use logic to figure out the answer to the whodunit.

Chapter 13

Get Inspired with Entertaining TV Shows and Films

Realistic

No legal drama is 100% accurate in its depiction of the law; they're not C-SPAN. That said, some shows get closer than others, weaving in realistic difficulties like lack of evidence, unreliable witnesses, and even social and political influences that can impact the tenor of a trial.

The Practice, which aired from 1997 to 2004, is often cited as one of the more realistic legal dramas. This television drama attempted to show a more realistic version of the law, taking inspiration from current cases, and exploring social themes, ethics, and morality. *The Practice* would become the blueprint for later shows like *The Good Wife* (2009–2016), which some call the most realistic scripted legal drama.

Another good example of a realistic legal drama is *Perry Mason*. The original, which debuted in 1957, followed the popular criminal defense lawyer at the height of his career, while the 2020 remake starts at the beginning, as Mason fumbles his way through his first case.

Entertaining

Popular television shows about the law include:

1. *Law & Order* - This long-running crime and legal drama series follows the investigations and trials of criminal cases in New York City.

2. *Suits* - This legal drama series revolves around a talented college dropout who starts working as a law associate for a high-profile lawyer despite never having attended law school.

3. *How to Get Away with Murder* - This suspenseful legal drama follows a criminal defense professor and her students, who become entangled in a murder plot.

4. *Better Call Saul* - This prequel to *Breaking Bad* follows the story of Jimmy McGill, a small-time lawyer struggling to

make a name for himself before becoming the morally ambiguous attorney, Saul Goodman.

5. *The Good Wife* - This legal and political drama series follows the life of Alicia Florrick, a lawyer and wife of a disgraced politician, as she restarts her legal career after her husband's scandal.

6. *Boston Legal* - This comedic legal drama series features a group of eccentric lawyers at a Boston law firm, tackling both high-profile and personal cases.

7. *Law & Order: Special Victims Unit* - This spin-off of the original *Law & Order* focuses on the investigations and prosecutions of crimes involving sexual assault and other serious offenses.

8. *The Practice* - This legal drama series follows a group of lawyers at a Boston law firm as they handle controversial and high-stakes cases.

9. *Damages* - This legal thriller series follows the intense legal battles between a ruthless lawyer and her protégé, as they navigate complex cases and personal vendettas.

10. *Ally McBeal* - This quirky legal comedy-drama series follows the professional and personal life of a young lawyer working at a Boston law firm, known for its eccentric attorneys and unusual cases.

These are just a few examples, but there are many other TV shows that explore legal themes and the practice of law.

On the Big Screen

Here are some popular movies about the law:

1. *To Kill a Mockingbird* (1962) - Based on Harper Lee's novel, this film follows a small-town lawyer defending a Black man accused of rape in 1930s Alabama.

2. *12 Angry Men* (1957) - This classic courtroom drama depicts the deliberations of a jury as they decide the fate of a young man accused of murder.

3. *A Few Good Men* (1992) - In this legal thriller, a military lawyer defends two marines charged with the murder of a fellow soldier.

4. *Legally Blonde* (2001) - This comedy follows a fashion-conscious sorority girl who enrolls in Harvard Law School to win back her ex-boyfriend and ends up discovering her own legal skills.

5. *Philadelphia* (1993) - Tom Hanks plays a gay lawyer with AIDS who sues his former law firm for discrimination in this powerful drama.

6. *My Cousin Vinny* (1992) - This comedy follows a novice lawyer who must defend his cousin and his friend in a murder trial in rural Alabama.

7. *The Verdict* (1982) - Paul Newman stars as a down-and-out lawyer who takes on a medical malpractice case against a powerful hospital in this legal drama.

8. *Erin Brockovich* (2000) - Based on a true story, this film follows a legal assistant who uncovers a massive environmental cover-up and fights against a corporation on behalf of affected residents.

9. *Inherit the Wind* (1960) - This courtroom drama is a fictionalized account of the famous Scopes Monkey Trial, which debated the teaching of evolution in schools.

10. *The Lincoln Lawyer* (2011) - Matthew McConaughey portrays a criminal defense attorney who operates out of his Lincoln Town Car and finds himself in a high-stakes case.

These are just a few examples, but there are many other movies that explore legal themes and the practice of law. Many of these movies are available ON DEMAND and on streaming services.

Chapter 14

Resources Within the Law

Stay Connected

Once you have graduated and received your law degree, there are various organizations that lawyers can join to enhance their professional development, network with other legal professionals, and stay updated on the latest legal trends and issues.

Some of these organizations include:

1. **American Bar Association (ABA):** The largest voluntary professional association for lawyers in the U.S., offering resources, networking opportunities, and continuing legal education programs.

2. **Corporate Counsel Women of Color (CCWC):** A support network for in-house women of color attorneys to promote national and international advancement in

the legal profession and workplace. Components involve substantive programming, networking, research gathering, and communicating.

3. **Federal Bar Association (FBA)**: An organization for federal practitioners, including judges, attorneys, and law students, promoting the sound administration of justice and professional excellence.

4. organization for legal practitioners, bar associations, and law societies, promoting international legal standards and facilitating professional development and networking.

5. **International Organizations:** Lawyers interested in international law can join organizations like the International Law Association (ILA) or the International Association of Young Lawyers (AIJA) to connect with legal professionals from around the world and engage in international legal issues.

6. **Legal Aid Organizations:** Lawyers interested in providing pro bono legal services can join organizations like the Legal Aid Society or Volunteer Lawyers Network to help underserved populations access legal representation.

7. **National Bar Association (NBA):** The oldest and largest national association of predominantly African-American lawyers and judges, focusing on promoting diversity and equality within the legal profession.

8. **State Bar Associations:** Each state in the U.S. has its own bar association, which lawyers can join to access resources, networking events, and continuing legal education specific to their jurisdiction.

9. **Women's Bar Associations:** Numerous local, state, and national organizations exist to support and empower women in the legal profession, such as the National Association of Women Lawyers (NAWL) and

the Women's Bar Association of the District of Columbia.

These are just a few examples of the many organizations available for lawyers to join. The choice of organization often depends on the lawyer's practice area, interests, and professional goals.

Photo Credits

Page 2
Photo of Man Talking to a Group
123rfID :rawpixel

Page 4
Group Talking With Scales of Justice
123rfID: armmypicca

Page 7
LSAT Test Bubble
Rattanasiri Inpinta

Page 11
Lecture Hall
Stock Club Nation: Mxtofpe

Page 15
Law School Building
123rfID: Ingus Kruklitis

Page 19
Careers in Health Care
123rfID: Kwanchai Lerttanapunyaporn

Page 21
Family Law
123rfID: Vitaliy Vodolazskyy

Page 23
Photo of the Scales of Justice
Stock Club Nation: Martinlwe

Page 25
Lady Scales of Justice
123rfID: studioeast

Page 27
STEM Collage
123rfID: Rashad Ashurov

Page 28
Cybersecurity
123rfID: Daniil Peshkov

Page 32
Law Firm Meeting (with African American Speaking)
123rfID: ufabizphoto

Page 36
Money
123rfID: Timis Nicoara

Page 37
Group of People Sitting at Office table
123rfID: Pitinan

Page 40
Debate Photo
Stock Club Nation: phiroxie

Page 44
Chess Board
123rfID: Parinya Lertwattanasakul

Page 46
Watching TV
123rfID: Stokkete

Page 51
US National Achieves
123rfID: Andrea Izzotti

Page 52
Photo of College Kids Cap and Gown
123rfID: Kasper Ravlo

ABOUT THE AUTHOR

Laurie Robinson Haden is the President and CEO of Corporate Counsel Women of Color (CCWC). In 2004, Laurie founded CCWC to advance women of color attorneys and foster diversity in the legal profession. She formerly worked for 18 years in multiple leadership roles at the CBS Corporation (now media and entertainment juggernaut Paramount+), including Senior Vice President and Assistant General Counsel of Litigation. *Savoy* magazine has recognized her as one of the country's "Most Influential Black Lawyers."

Laurie and her husband, David Haden, have recently launched a 501 (c) (3) nonprofit foundation, Parents Supporting Excellence in Education, in Prince George's County, Maryland, where they partner with area schools in their community to provide equal educational access and resources to students. For seven years, Laurie was a NAACP Legal Defense

Fund board member. She serves on the Board of Visitors of Indiana University Maurer School of Law at Bloomington and North Carolina Central School of Law, where she served as chair (2022-2023) and is on the Compensation Committee of the National Sales Network. Laurie is the author *of It's Time to Shine: A Guide for Professionals of Color on How to Advance Their Career.* Laurie earned her Bachelor of Arts from North Carolina Central University (magna cum laude) and her Juris Doctor from the Indiana University Maurer School of Law at Bloomington.

Laurie@laurierobinsonhaden.com
Website: https://laurierobinsonhaden.com/

Laurie Robinson Haden

Made in the USA
Middletown, DE
14 April 2024

53009974R00035